Authentic Autistic Living

Michelle Swan

Books in the "Living Autistically" series:

Fierce Autistic Heart   (2024)
Authentic Autistic Living   (2024)
Perfectly Normal Autistic   (2024)

Original cover art by Emory Thorsen.

ISBN 978-0-6488711-5-6 (print - paperback)
ISBN 978-0-6488711-9-4 (EPUB)
ISBN 978-0-9756585-1-2 (PDF)

Published in Australia by Michelle Swan
© Michelle Swan 2024
This work is copyright. Apart from any use permitted under the Copyright Act 1968, no part may be reproduced by any process, nor may any other exclusive right be exercised, without the permission of the author.
contact@hellomichelleswan.com

This book is for informational purposes only. It does not constitute advice, and should not be used as replacement for professional support and/or diagnosis.

This book is dedicated to
the wonderful friends in my life
who have contributed to my ever evolving
understanding of myself.

contents

introduction	i
burnout	1
anxiety	8
fear	18
stress	22
scared	28
overwhelmed	31
meltdown	36
shutdown	42
trauma	45
wonky	50
rest	58
flow	61
interests	66
indistinguishability	73
crying	78
disabled	81
identity	85
authentic	90

introduction

This book is the second of three in my series, Living Autistically. In the first, "Fierce Autistic Heart", I shared with you how I came to understand myself as Autistic, and began to learn to like myself. In this book I am sharing thoughts on living authentically as an Autistic person.

Authenticity is a prized characteristic. Popular psychology talks about authenticity often, and encourages us to be authentic at all costs… even sometimes in what I would call ruthless and unconsidered ways. I am not interested in living without intent, or in ways that may sabotage my desire to live well. So I have done a lot thinking on what it means for me to live authentically.

The world is a very noisy place, and there are a lot of very strong opinions available to us that, if we choose to, we can use to inform our decisions about what authenticity is. If we aren't very careful we can accidentally find ourselves merely copying what we think other people expect of us rather than actually identifying what is right for us.

Authenticity is an individual thing, not a group state.

For a neurodivergent person attempting to find our own state of authenticity in this very noisy world requires us to separate ourselves from mainstream thought and practice for long enough to get in touch with our own bodies unique needs and to experiment with our own self care practice.

I've written, in this book, some of my own experience and process of discovering how I can live authentically. I'm sharing it with you in the hope that there will be something here that helps you realise what authenticity can look like for you personally.

Michelle

burnout

I thought I was depressed. I was told by medical professionals that I had depression. Looking back now, I can easily recognise that what I was experiencing was autistic burn out. When I look back over the years of my young adulthood I can see clearly that burn out and I have co existed for quite some time.

There are periods where, in retrospect, it is quite obvious that I was burnt out. It didn't occur to me at the time that my fantasies of walking out the door away from my life and never returning were symptoms of my lack of coping strategies. It didn't seem so odd to me back then to think how nice it wold be to fall asleep and never wake again. Fortunately the time I found myself counting tablets I had both the good friends to support me and the good sense to call them.

There were times I battled on, sleeping on the sofa in the day time while the children played and watched tv, then laying awake at night wondering what my problem was and why I couldn't just snap out of it.

Years have passed, and burn out is often close. I was for a time using anti depressant medication to help manage it. It only sort of worked. There is a combination of numbness and brain fog that comes with burn out, that means it's so difficult to make decisions, and do just the basics of every day living, even though I might want to.

These days I can recognise the signs in myself and I have a plan and strategies I use to make sure I do not allow myself to fall back into the foggy hole that sometimes calls.

It might sound strange, but there are days when the effort to take care of myself is great and the temptation to slide away for a while is strong. It's not that I like the fog, it just sometimes seems easier to go there than to fight it. I am careful to not get too close to the edge. I am careful not to flirt with it too much.

When I notice the signs I am moving closer, I limit my social exposure, I don't push myself to maintain a perfect house, I make sure to write down the things that are bothering me so my mind can shelve them instead of lugging them around all the time taking up all my emotional energy, I talk to my trusted support people.

Many years ago a doctor told me that when you live with a lot of stress reactive depression is a normal and understandable response, but that I have so much insight and I cope so well. She says it would be more unexpected if I didn't feel overwhelmed sometimes. And that might all be true, but the years have taught me that I cannot just snap out of it, so I must not get into it…. I must care for myself first. I have realised that what looks like depression to some, in me is having pushed through overwhelm too long and becoming a burnt out autistic person.

When I vanish online for a while it is usually because I must, in order to avoid being in that place of having done too much.

When I take too long to respond to a message or text, or when I fail to answer the phone, it is usually because I do not have the emotional energy to process a response.

When I turn down an invitation it is usually not because I don't want to go out or be around people, but because I simply can't manage to do anything other than care for my immediate needs and those of my family.

When I seem aloof and a bit too much like I have it all together, it is often because if I give in to a negative thought process I know I will stay there for too long and not be able to pull myself out.

Burn out is not something that is inherently bad. The realisation that I am often so close to it neither upsets or surprises me.
It just is.

When I am burnt out I need to be aware that I require extra time to get things done, I need more time to process new information and to recall old information, I need to be gentle with my expectations of myself. My executive function is certainly compromised, and I need more sleep than usual. I find all that manageable, and as long as my energy levels stay where I find those things manageable there is no problem.

The thing that becomes dangerous for me when I am burnt out is discontent. When I allow myself to focus on discontent, I find myself becoming even more easily overwhelmed. When I am really overwhelmed I do not look after myself and remember to be more gentle and mindful with my expectations of what I can realistically get done in a day.

If I allow myself to focus on discontent, it is very easy to slip into a negative thought spiral. Overwhelm keeps great company with thoughts of inadequacy, and is best friends with the thought spiral that starts with comparing myself with others. I am not on top of things, I am not supporting my family, the house is a wreck, I am not young enough, pretty enough, confident enough, organised enough, just not enough of anything. And so the spiral goes down down down, until I am so deep in it I can barely remember the things I **can** do well enough to glimpse the top of the funnel I just slid down.

So, what is the solution? Well, for me it involves a few things.

I am very careful with my words in public. I make a conscious decision to focus on the positive and avoid dwelling on the negative when it comes to reporting my own experiences. This is because I believe giving voice to the nagging negative thoughts reinforces them and gives them strength. That is not to say I don't ever speak negatively. I do. I choose my friends carefully, and have a couple of trusted friends who I know will listen with empathy and encourage me. Sometimes I need to be called out if I am losing my way, sometimes firmly, sometimes with just a little humour.

I am careful to recognise the early signs that I am in need of a break from social and emotional stimulation, and I take a break. Things that trigger me can be in real face to face life, or in real online life. I give myself frequent minimal social media days (not ideal from a professional perspective but essential for my health!) and I ration out my local socialising hours as well.

I am careful to do things just for myself. I love to be in nature. I love taking photos. I like walking, being in the water and practicing karate. Those things interrupt a negative though cycle so effectively and provide an opportunity for me to reset my focus away from discontent.

While those strategies sound simple, and they are, they are not always easy. When you are caring for a large family with multiple extra challenges and a variety of support needs, focussing on self care is often the last thing on the list of each days "to do's". But it is so important. I don't claim to be perfect at this, but I am certainly a lot better at looking after myself than I used to be. Sometimes it helps to think of it as looking after my family by looking after myself- if I am not coping I am no use to them! Ultimately, though, there is nothing wrong with self care just because you care about yourself. Whatever self talk I need to use to ensure I do actually look after myself, avoiding wallowing in discontent and getting lost in negative thought spirals is crucial to me.

anxiety

Some days I'm a weird mix of tired and anxious. I'm not worried about anything in particular, but everything worries me and it's hard to make a decision about anything. I'm not physically sick, but there is a queasiness in my stomach and a feeling in my chest. I am tired and foggy in my brain, but I don't want to lie down to rest because that it exactly when my brain will jump into action and I will feel worse.

On days like this I don't get anything done other than things I absolutely can't avoid. If the day is one with nothing much I can't avoid I manage to get through okay. If the day is one in which I have multiple drop off an pick ups to do for the children, appointments to keep, food shopping to do, dinner to organise, and still find energy to go to karate…. well, on those days I find myself sitting in my chair at 5.15pm desperately in need of both a drink and a visit to the bathroom but unable to do anything until I have cleared my mind of the thoughts that are bothering me even though I really should be onto making dinner by now.

These are the days I actually feel like I have taken on too much and probably should not be a parent. No one is starving or in any danger, but I feel woefully incompetent.

5.18pm and I feel like I could go to bed and stay there until morning…. but bedtime is about 5 hours away. And I felt like this 5 hours ago.

If I have more than a couple of days in a row like this I start cancelling things. I have to if I don't want to end up shut down for a few days. The house gets messier and messier. Dirty clothes and dishes pile up. If it goes on too long it takes me weeks to catch up.
Some weeks I don't have any days like this. Some weeks I have more days like this than not. Sometimes I have a week full of days like this.

Sometimes I don't really seem to catch up… or I almost get there and then I'm slipping again. Falling behind again.

5.24pm and my body just remembered to tell me I am really hungry now. I still haven't been able to empty my mind enough to get up. It's a bit like I imagine a locked up computer would feel if it had feelings.

If I make the mistake of looking at the calendar for the next day I can do nothing I know I'll feel worse because this is a busy week.

If I make a quick easy dinner instead of the one I bought ingredients for I will get through the evening more easily. Better still I can ask one of the older kids to do the quick dinner. Remembering I can ask for help is a skill I am still learning. Delegation is an important self care skill- note to self! Dinner sorted, now I can clear a space to think about karate. I like karate, it will be fine. When I get back the children will be about ready for bed. I can go to bed early and ignore the dishes a while longer. I have plan. Now I can go to the bathroom and have a drink.

I feel like it would seem silly to others, but this is how my mind works and how my days often look. Tired and anxious, almost burnt out but not quite. Taking frequent breaks to clear my thoughts so I can move on with the day. Almost not coping. Or almost doing well. Depending on how you look at it.

Take a deep breath and smile. One foot in front of the other until I can stop.

It's not a crisis. I'm not stressed, or in pain. I don't need saving or even sympathy. It just is.

My life.

I'm not complaining. I'm just saying. I think sometimes it's this sort of thing they are talking about when they say everyone is fighting a battle you know nothing about. I mean, sometimes they are talking about death or illness, or tragedy or big stuff. But sometimes it's this… just life for some people. I know there are others like me. It's not just my story.

Other days I am more on top of things, more able to read my own emotions, and better able to deliberately manage my anxiety.

I have learned that fear and anxiety often feel the same.

Fear is there for a good reason, and we should pay attention to it because it helps us look after ourselves and stay safe. It is good to listen to our fears and adjust our behaviour accordingly. Fear should be respected.

Anxiety is not so reasonable, and is an over reaction to a situation that happens internally, so some say. I am learning to think of my anxiety slightly differently than we are often told to. I understand it with alternate nuance through a lens of neurodivergence. I think anxiety, like almost everything, exists on a continuum. A little can be helpful because we can use it as motivation, to help us meet a deadline, for example. But too much anxiety- let to grow unchecked breeds rumination and inaction and puts us on the unhealthy end of the continuum. We should be careful about listening to our anxiety because it can push us to do things that aren't good for us in the long term. Anxiety does need management.

It is important to know if we are feeling fearful or anxious, because that knowledge helps us know how to respond. It can be very difficult to differentiate anxiety from fear, because it feels very similar. Especially when you have quite likely been told you are anxious when you are actually feeling fear.

In the moment, the raised heart rate, the shallow breathing, the racing thoughts, don't always let us know whether it is fear or anxiety we are dealing with. We have to do some thinking.

Unfortunately, times when we are fearful or anxious are precisely the times thinking is hardest!

There is a difference between a reaction and a response. The reaction is often an emotion or a feeling. Sometimes we allow our behaviour to be a reaction too. But if we behaviourally react to an anxiety, we can accidentally reinforce it. So, when we are not in immediate danger, it is a good idea to wait until the emotional reaction passes before deciding on a considered behavioural response.

This is when distraction is helpful. All emotions pass after a while. Even if we do nothing about them, they build, peak, break and recede, just like a wave. If we can wait until that happens it is easier to have a think about what is happening. Distracting and waiting out the emotional reaction gives us the opportunity to choose a response that is more likely to be in our long term best interest.

Let me say again though, if there is immediate danger, distracting isn't okay. Immediate danger probably means you are feeling fear, and you should do something now!

Once you have distracted, and waited out the passing of the emotional reaction, you can think more clearly and choose a response. Your response will be based on whether you are fearful or anxious.

If you are fearful, you will choose to respond by taking steps to keep yourself safe (more on that next chapter).

If you are anxious you will want to respond by breaking the anxiety cycle and working toward teaching your brain that the situation you are in is not one that requires you to be stressed. This is a process that will usually require the help of a competent mental health professional.

I am not a mental health professional. I am an Autistic advocate who lives with high levels of anxiety. This chapter is not giving you professional mental health advice. It is sharing with you what I know and what works for me.

To break my anxiety cycle I do the following things:

- I start by distracting until the biggest emotions that stop me from thinking logically have passed. But I am careful that I am not distracting for too long. Distracting is things like playing games on the phone or reading. These distract your mind, but don't change what your body is doing. If our body still feels stressed and doesn't get a signal to not be stressed, we stay stressed.

- Once I am not in reaction mode, I allow myself to feel the feeling so I can move on to heal (ignoring my feelings in the short term makes them bigger in the long term)

- I use some self regulation strategies to give myself the best chance of making logical and healthy choices. Self regulation is things like big movement stimming, singing, walking, running or other exercise that gets you out of breath. Things that let your body shift what it is doing… engage your vagus nerve, trigger your nervous system to behave differently.

- Then I talk through my anxiety and challenge it. This process is different depending on what the anxiety is about. It might involve "what's the worst that can happen?" questioning (this one is risky if the anxiety is based on a real fear, so I have to be careful!). It might involve "I have done everything I need to and can rest now" self talk. It might involve "it is likely you have misread the situation and this is an overreaction" observations and reassurance.

- After I challenge my anxiety I choose a behavioural response that suits the situation. Sometimes I choose to do nothing. Sometimes I choose to talk to someone close to me about how I am feeling. Sometimes I choose to change something about my environment. Sometimes I choose to note that I am going to need more help from a professional and I record the situation to talk with my therapist about later.

Remember that everyone processes their fear and anxiety in slightly different ways, and those ways are influenced by past trauma and life experiences. What works for me won't work in exactly the same way for everyone. You will need to use some trial and error in figuring out your own individual strategies, and that takes time and energy. Be kind to yourself as you work through it.

fear

When I was writing about anxiety I mentioned that it is possible to be told you are experiencing anxiety when what you are experiencing is fear. I'd like to explain that in more detail here.

I am afraid of going to the shops.

Most people would assume that I don't want to go to the shops because of anxiety. But my aversion to the shops is not unreasonable or out of proportion in relation to my experience of being in the shops.

The shopping environment is physically painful for me. The bright lights, the loud noises, the closeness of other people, the visually overstimulating arrangement of countless brightly labelled products, managing an unruly shopping trolley, the frustration of not being able to find the item I need, the sense of impending decision fatigue. All these things overwhelming to the point of physical discomfort in my abdomen and in my head.

When I say I am afraid of going to the shops it is because it's a normal human response to the anticipation of pain to feel fear.

If your experience of going to the shops isn't the same as mine you are quite likely have trouble understanding, without me providing detailed information, that I experience fear of going to the shops. You are more likely to assume that I'm anxious, because that makes no sense to somebody who doesn't experience pain from going shopping.

If I was experiencing anxiety about going to the shops it would quite likely motivate me towards rumination and inaction. My fear of going to the shops, on the other hand, motivates me to problem solve and come up with ways I can go to the shops without experiencing so much pain.
I choose the times that I go to the shops carefully, aiming to be there when I know there won't be as many people, at times of day or when the shelves I'm more likely to be fully stocked, and I shop at places where I am familiar with the layout of the store, taking a well planned List that is laid out

with items in the order that I will pass them as I walk through the shop. I almost always wear my sunglasses well I'm shopping, and on days when I have to go shopping but I'm already a bit overwhelmed I will wear my noise cancelling headphones.

Fears purpose is to give us information about what we need protection from. Ignoring fear is unwise and can be reckless.

A lot of autistic and neurodivergent people have a pretty complicated relationship with their fear. In large part this is because when we were younger and we felt fear it was labelled by others as anxiety. We have learnt to distrust our own internal nervous system cues that were trying to tell us that we needed protection. Unfortunately this often leads to shame.

For me a lot of the work I had to do in order to become comfortable acknowledging and meeting my own needs was to learn not to be ashamed of having different experiences and therefore different needs and the people around me. Allowing myself to feel my fear, and letting it guide me, means I can make healthier decisions about my own self care. Making healthier decisions about my own self care means I can live a better life.

stress

I have spent a lot of time learning to manage stress in my life. Before I explain how, let's make sure we all understand what I mean when I say stress. I feel like societally we understand stress as an inherently negative thing. That is not the way I see it. I see stress as anything that creates a sense of tension or brings on a state of tiredness leading to overwhelm. Some stress is from things that are necessary in our lives, and some we can choose to avoid. Some stress comes from negative experiences, but some comes from positive experiences.

Some examples of what I think of as negative stress (not an exhaustive list):
* facing other peoples biases as an obstacle to having success in advocacy situations
* dealing with people who are rude, inconsiderate, and bigoted or discriminatory
* coping with environments that are sensorily hostile or inaccessible to my family

* physical illness, injury, and pain

Some examples of what I think of as positive stress (also not an exhaustive list):
* spending time in small groups with friends and family
* gardening
* karate training
* travelling to new and unknown places
* mentoring and advocacy work

The difference in the two categories is mostly about what I get from them. The negative stress situations only drain me and cost me more than I can possibly receive from them. The positive stress situations drain me in some ways, but they also feed me in that I gain positive things from them that outweigh the costs of participating in the activities.

I'm going to expand on the example of karate training. There are physical, mental, emotional, sensory, social, and time related stressors involved in attending regular training. These things certainly all take their toll on me. However, I also enjoy karate. I gain a feeling of confidence and satisfaction when I master a technique, learn a new kata, face my fears in competition, and push my body to become more fit. I find the effort I put in for the hour and a half training session forces me to focus only on what I am doing (otherwise I'd fall over or hurt myself), so it helps me clear my mind of all other things for a while and acts as a kind of reset mentally for me. I am spending time with others who enjoy the same activity as me, and who encourage me and who I can encourage. It is an environment that is predictable and positive and in which I am valued and can add value.

In the example of facing other peoples biases as an obstacle to having success in advocacy situations, I simply find this draining. It is a situation that repeats itself over and over again, and even though I must deal with it, it sucks my energy and coping skills if I have to engage with it. It is predictable in its monotony and in its outcomes, and although some predictability can be good, in this context it is not. Being faced with the ugliness of what some people truly think about families like mine is not something I get anything positive from.

What I have learned to carefully consider when I plan my week, and as I make decisions
when situations arise that require my attention, is whether I am balancing my need for self

protection, self regulation and recovery time in good proportion with the stress I undertake to include in my life. This applies to both the negative stressors and the positive stressors.

I make decisions on an ongoing basis about how much negative stress I am willing to expose myself to, how much positive stress I can include, and how much down time I must include in order to stay healthy and able to do the things life requires of me.

This can be hard. Sometimes it does mean saying no to things I would have liked to do. It is particularly hard when something out of my control from the negative stress category steals energy away and means I have to say no to some positive stress things that I wanted to do.

If I am careful to keep a good balance of stress and rest in my life, over time I seem to be able to handle more negative stress before it overwhelms me. I do still find there is a point where I have to make a decision to avoid most stress (positive and negative) for a while every now and then. When that happens I just have a nothing day or two.

Nothing days are when I do only the essentials- drop children at school and activities, make sure everyone eats and everyone is safe. On these days I will actively do things to keep my brain from engaging with things that will mentally drain me (so no social media!), and make an effort to only engage with what is literally in front of me. I try to stay home, even in bed if I can (not possible with children really, but even an hour here and there helps me reset), and rest both physically and mentally.

In the past I have just pushed myself through stress, to the point of exhaustion that required medical support to rectify. I have been so underweight I was unhealthy, I have been diagnosed with depression, I have been through periods of insomnia, all because I pushed hard and didn't listen when my body said stop.

Listening to my body and being aware of how stress impacts on me has been a life changer for me. People didn't know I wasn't coping because I hid all my stress inside myself, to my own detriment. They didn't realise how difficult I find sensory stimulation and social situations. Now people still don't realise, but it is not because I am hiding and not coping in private- it is because I am self caring in private, and so I am coping better with life. That's a thing I am proud to have learned.

scared

"I thought you were angry."
It's a phrase I've become used to hearing.
"Why are you angry?"
I guess it's a fair enough assumption.
My voice was raised. My words were strong. My body language was not relaxed or calm.

You see, there is so much going on inside that I can't explain in the moment. I can sometimes manage to say things like "I don't like that", "it's too much", "it's too hard", and "stop".

Sometimes I can't say anything and I just go quiet. I know my jaw is clenched and my shoulders are hunched. I might walk away, or sit in stony silence. Lots of people do look like that when they are angry.

When you reacted as though I was angry, when you told me "don't be angry", I thought that maybe I was angry. I thought you were right. I believed you for a while. But when I thought about it later, when I had the strength to deal with my discomfort and think about what was really happening for me, I realised you were wrong.

To a small degree I was angry. And frustrated. And a bit annoyed. But mostly? Mostly I was scared.

I am experiencing lots of things you can't see: sensory overload– the way the sounds hurt my body, the way the light makes it hard to think, the way the smells are distracting me.

language processing difficulty- the way my brain is unable to put the words you are saying into sentences I can understand, the feeling of knowing what I want to say but not being able to find the right words to use.

anxious thoughts– past experiences of stress and other peoples reactions to me when I am stressed, knowing that if I push myself too hard or am pushed too much by someone else I will become overloaded, the recurring thoughts of not being good enough strong enough capable enough.

These things all combine so that when I am in a situation that is unexpected, surprising, stressful or unsettling, I get scared.

I am scared that I won't know what to do. Scared that I will do the wrong thing. Scared that you will think I am silly, incapable, over-reacting, under-reacting, or any number of other things I don't want you to think. I'm scared that if I can't quickly get control over myself, my body and how I feel, that I am going to cry or yell or curse, or worse… have a meltdown in front of you.

I am scared that you've noticed I am stressed and you are going to want me to explain why. You might ask if you can help, and then I will have to choose between appearing cold or making myself more vulnerable to you, and I don't know you well enough to know if I can trust you. Or if I do know you and trust you I am sacred that if I do tell you what's happening you won't know what to do and you will be uncomfortable and then I'll feel like I have to comfort you when I can't even look after myself just now.

You might think I look angry, but I'm really not. I am scared.

overwhelmed

For an Autistic person, the world is often just simply too much.

Too bright, too loud, too fast, too close, too intense.

One way to manage the overwhelm is to hide away and completely control the input. But this strategy is not realistic. Aside from needing to work, and buy food, autistic people do need to connect with other people, despite what the stereotypes might ask you to believe.

Another way to manage overwhelm is to stim. Everyone stims. It's not an Autistic only thing. Pen clicking, knuckle cracking, leg bouncing, hair twirling, nail biting…. it's all stimming and we all use it for self regulation.

Many autistic people do tend stim more often and in less subtle ways than non-autistic people. I guess that is largely because we experience the sensory world more intensely than others, so we have a greater need for regulation.

I spend so much of my time in public **not stimming**. I really wish I was more comfortable letting others see me move the way I want to, and need to.

I know it would allow me to stress release as I go through my day and mean I would need less recovery time at the end of the day.

My hands want to move, shake, flap, tap my fingertips against each other in rhythmic sequences, make patterns on my face, twist my hair.

My feet want to wiggle, bounce my legs, push down on their own sides and feel that firm pressure.

My shoulders want to move, to hunch up and down. Tight, loose, tight, loose.

My hips want to sway, soothing and steady, side to side.

But instead I sit on my hands, plant my feet flat, stand still, and conform.

I feel cross and disappointed with myself.

"It is okay to need to move" I tell everyone else. Yet I do not often allow myself that same permission.

My internal voice says "sit still", "concentrate", "don't fidget", "BE STILL".

The more stressed I am the less I listen to that voice. Sometimes, I find myself tapping my fingers. Sometimes, I stop when I notice I am doing it. Sometimes I let myself go. No one has ever commented, or asked me about it. So why am I so self conscious?

Why don't I let myself stim in front of other people most of the time?
It's fear.

Fear that someone will notice. Fear that they will think differently of me. Fear they will pass judgement about the way my body moves. Fear they will comment about it. Fear I will not know what to say if they comment.

I am scared to stim in obvious ways in front of others.

They probably haven't done anything directly to make me scared to stim in front of them. They would probably tell me that they don't mind if I do what I need to feel grounded and regulated. They would likely tell me I don't need to feel scared. But have they done anything to help me feel safe?

For Autistic people to feel safe stimming noticeably in public, we need other people to help us challenge societies expectation of normality. We need people to be vocal about the value of diversity. To celebrate difference by sharing the words of people from minority groups. We need people to be active in defending the bullied and marginalised.
But too often people use words like disorder and deficit when they talk about children, adults, families like mine. Children are told they need to be still, concentrate, stop wiggling. People stay silent when they see marginalised groups begging for their rights to be upheld.

If autistic people have any hope of the overwhelm we experience being reduced, we need changes to be made to the environment around us, and we need our coping strategies to be normalised. If they are not normalised we will continue to be overwhelmed.

meltdown

everything is suddenly louder. it was loud before but now it's like there is an extra megaphone inside my head and it hurts when a sound flows through it. hurts in my whole body. right to my core. and ricocheting back out again to my skin.

the sound is slower somehow. but piercing. the words are clear but I can't sort them out, so I can't answer. the only words I can find are "I need a minute" but they aren't true. I actually need you to not talk to me at all for the next hour or more. I don't really know how long it will be until I can think in words again, but it isn't now.

you are trying to help because you care and you can tell something is wrong. I know you think you know what is wrong, and you are right that what you saw happen was part of it, but in truth it is a small part. that is just what happened outside my body. the real challenge is getting through what is happening in here that no one else can see or hear or feel and that I can't explain.

I don't want to cry where everyone can see me. but stopping myself from letting tears fall makes me feel worse. I know I'm trying to hold back the tide, but I try. defiantly ignoring my needs until they cannot be stopped.

my skin feels wrong. it feels electric. it tingles and burns and hurts. the air on me is too much. my clothes are heavy and hot. my head is a boulder and floating at the same time. my ears and eyes and limbs and pores are full to overflowing with everything and nothing and more.

my body feels wrong. my arms are awkward and uncomfortable. my legs ache and want to keep moving. my hips stiff. my neck sore and tight. everything poised wanting to run somewhere. anywhere else.

my thoughts feel wrong. jumbled. foggy. frightened even though I know there is no real danger. overwhelmed. racing without words and with no direction. fast and wild. out of control.

I am trying to find something to ground myself. I'm trying to think of what I need. I have some words but they won't come out my mouth, and if they did they wouldn't be enough to help you know what I need and I would feel shame at my inability to articulate what is happening for me.

I need to be home now. but home is far away and I can't get there on my own. I know my reactions are mechanical, automatic, but not flowing. I have to stop. there is no option because I can't think anymore. I take myself somewhere away from everyone and everything to try to stop the assault of sensory information hurtling at me. away from sounds, voices, questions. away from help. I hide.

I am screaming. I can feel it in my throat and hear the sound fill the air around me.

I am crying. I can feel my lungs expel then inhale great gulps of air. I can feel my shoulders heave and my whole body shudder.

I am shaking. not in my hands or shoulders or legs, but inside all of me. trembling and twitching from the inside even though I look still. I can hear my voice telling me I am ok. I don't quite believe me.

I am exhausted. but still not safe. the ground is solid I know, but it is not the anchor I need. I need the release of nothing. of quiet solitude in my own safe space. the calming pressure of blankets over my body. the welcome of closed eyes. the soothing release of sleep.

it feels like forever. the clock says it is twenty minutes.

I am spinning inside my head. my vision is dark. I need to slow my breath down. exhale. find something to hold in my hand and squeeze hard on. I need to move, to sway, to rock. but I know I have no balance just now.

sit. exhale. inhale. one. breath. at. a .time. slowly. gradually. calming. breathing. in. out.

I am tired. sleepy. still foggy. but not panicked. my thoughts try to return. I feel outside myself. observing. soothing. reassuring. my eyes still wet with tears. my face swollen. my everything raw and vulnerable.

slowly. gradually. calming. breathing. in. out.

if you know me and I trust you to see me exposed, you can sit with me now, still and without touching or demanding, and I can being to relax.

if I trust you, your presence begins to calm the storm in my body and mind. sometimes, most times, just your presence is enough. being there for me when I am at my most vulnerable and allowing me to sense your calm is a gift. I feel your calm move through the space between us and I can hold it as my own until I can re-centre myself and stand alone again.

and time passes. I begin to feel it now.

if you come to me now with quiet simple words I can hear you and find a response. I still can't explain well but I might be able to tell you what I experienced, and I might be able to decide what I need to feel better.

with more time I can air my anxieties and fears. your acknowledgement of them as valid gives me peace to walk with them when I can't fight them off, your ability to hear them without mirroring my panic takes away their strength, your steady presence gives me strength to face them as my own panic recedes.

your acceptance of me in my weakness helps me to accept myself. your willingness to be with me when I feel unlovable allows me to see myself as important. your confidence to just be with me, without trying to fix anything, reassures me that you believe I am capable, even when I am overwhelmed and don't feel it myself.

shutdown

A build up of overwhelm approaching a meltdown can sometimes be avoided by internalising the discomfort. While a melt down is very externally focussed, a shut down takes all the pain and the outward evidence of it and turns it inward to simmer where others can't notice it until it subsides enough for outward behaviour to return to what is considered normal. Sometimes I can choose to shut down instead of meltdown. Sometimes a meltdown is inevitable.

Shutdown comes with a sense of shame, similar to meltdown. At the very least there is a feeling of wishing I wasn't here again.

Often for me shut down brings with it reduced or no capacity for spoken language (an experience known as situational mutism), and reduced or no capacity for movement. During a particularly intense shut down I will be stuck unable to speak or move. As you can imagine this level of internal distress can be quite frightening.

It's not that my mind is blank and I'm not having any thoughts during a shutdown, in fact I am often having quite complicated thoughts, it's just that I am completely unable to translate those thought concepts into words that I can speak with my mouth. If I haven't lost my capacity for movement I may be able to type them.

To an observer shutdown can look like defiance or deliberate non-compliance. Being misunderstood in this way during the shutdown increases the sense of overwhelm and it's very likely to prolong the period of time it takes to recover.

Shutdowns can also be cause by positive stressors. An intensely pleasurable experience can lead to enough overwhelm to induce a shut down. The shutdowns can be even more embarrassing because people are more likely to understand the shutdown that's resulted from a negative experience than a positive one.

Regardless of the cause, recovery from shutdown needs time and patience. If I'm experiencing shut down I do my best to find a quiet, reduced light, soft and cosy space to sit and rest, or sleep if possible, and wait until my nervous system is less activated and overwhelmed.

If I have a trusted and safe person with me it can help if they sit with me, give me a firm hug, and just wait quietly until I'm feeling recovered. During a shutdown I am unable to answer questions or explain what is happening, and I definitely can't make decisions about what I need other then to know I don't want anything that puts pressure on me to think or feel.

Approaching shutdowns with compassion and gentleness helps them to pass more quickly. Understanding shutdowns as a protective strategy helps them to be an experience that is more useful than shameful.

trauma

When I'm talking about meltdown and shutdown, I'm aware that I am also talking about nervous system dysregulation and, quite likely to some extent, trauma responses.

Flight, fight, freeze, and fawn are concepts more understood in the mainstream these days, thanks to popular psychology and the concepts being presented in social media. However, I would love to see a better societal understanding of what the neurodivergent experience of trauma is. I suspect that at times, what psychologists would call a freeze response in an autistic person may instead be a shutdown caused by overwhelm, and while many would argue these are the same thing, I see those two things as being somewhat different. I think that often when we say something is a freeze response there is an assumption that what caused it was "big", when I see an autistic shut down as often being caused more by a series of "small" things. Maybe I'm missing some important information, and I'm sure that my understanding of this will grow over time. I may be speaking too early in my understanding, but I felt it important to include some thoughts on the topic of trauma in this book.

Regardless of whether trauma responses and coping strategies like the 4 F's are the same as meltdowns and shutdowns…. I think it is important to realise that autistic people are more likely to be traumatised than non autistic people. I can see three reasons for this.

First I'll make an attempt to define trauma.

My understanding of trauma is that it is a dysregulation that occurs as a result of not having the capacity, or being supported well enough, to process difficult situations. The trauma isn't the actual situation or event, but what happens after by way of helping us to find or create a feeling of safety when something is happened that has compromised a felt sense of safety. Sometimes we can do that on our own, and sometimes we need help. If it happens that we need help and it isn't available we are more likely to remain in a state of dysregulation and feeling unsafe until we can somehow process or resolve what happened in a way that satisfies our need to feel safe. It is possible for two people to have the same experience and for only one of them to be traumatised by it. One of the key differences being that they received different support after the event. Of course it's more complicated than that, and many amazing minds have done a lot of learning in the space of understanding trauma so there is lots of great information available elsewhere. But I think the principles I outline here are enough of a basis to proceed.

So, what are the reasons autistic people are more likely to experience trauma than other people?

The first is that we are already super sensitive to external input and so are more likely to experience things as difficult and need support to manage our needs than non autistic people.

The second reason is that an autistic person's needs are very likely to be misunderstood by a non autistic person, and if someone doesn't understand what you need, they aren't going to be able to support you effectively.

The third reason is one I find more confronting. Autistic people are more likely to be in situations that are likely to cause trauma. Statistics show that autistic people are more likely to be abused than the general population. Some research indicates that autistic children are as much as three times more likely to be victims of bullying, physical abuse and sexual abuse. I don't know of any specific research that looks into the reasons why autistic people are targeted more often in these ways (if you do, I'd love you to let me know about it!). But the data is there that tells us some of the reason autistic people are more likely to be traumatised is they are more likely to be targets of abuse.

I found learning of these three reasons pretty sobering. And I wanted to know- what can I do to protect myself?

As with many of the questions I ask about life and living well, the answer I arrived at has been self awareness and self care.

I am responsible for looking after myself, so I must know what my needs are, where my limits are, and when I need support.

I must be aware enough of other people know who is safe to be around and who are the appropriate people to ask for support.

We guard ourselves against trauma by knowing who we are and what we need. And by being aware of who others are and what we can realistically and fair expect of and ask of them. These are skills that are learned, often through difficult experiences. They are rarely learned effectively through theoretical discussion- though discussion is a good way to plant information seeds that than be grown through experience. We cope best with difficult experiences if we have caring and accepting community around us.

wonky

Some days I wake up feeling good, I am productive and get to the end of the day still feeling pretty good. Some days I wake up feeling good, but somewhere along the way things go a bit off and I abandon plans in favour of resting to avoid overload. Some days I wake up and nothing feels right, the whole day is a struggle and the best way to describe how I feel is just "wonky". Wonky days are difficult to manage, but I am getting better at it.

I'll try to explain what I mean by "wonky". It's a feeling of something (or everything) being off, but not being able to identify exactly what is not right or needs attention in my body or mind in order to stop feeling off. Another word for it might be overwhelmed, but for me when I identify that I feel overwhelmed I can also name a trigger or cause. Wonky is just a pervasive feeling of "not right" without being able to easily identify a cause of it. A lot of the time wonky days happen when I am having executive functioning challenges or if I am experiencing increased sensory sensitivity.

I have a list of some of the things that I notice are often a problem for me so I can check in with myself to see what I can do to make things better when I feel wonky. In my head it is a bit like a mind map or flow chart, but for the purpose of sharing it with you I'll just put it here as a list of questions I ask myself, with explanations and solutions. This list is in the order I use to check in with myself. I do the checks in this order because it lists the checks in order of how likely they are to be the problem, with the most likely at the top.

Are you hungry or thirsty?

My body doesn't seem to tell me I am hungry until I am really really, trembling and nauseous hungry. Sometimes (most days!) I forget to eat, so taking a minute to think about when I last ate and if I might be hungry is helpful. When I am asked "are you hungry" my answer is often, "maybe a little" but then 5 minutes later I realise that actually I am really very hungry and I need to eat now. It's like the reminder triggers something in my brain that allows me to subconsciously process and then catch up with what my body is needing.

Do you have pain anywhere, or might you be injured?

To answer this I have to do an inventory of my body. I start at the top and think about my head then move down my body mentally checking to see if I have pain. It is fairly common for me to be experiencing pain but it not registering consciously unless it is significant or having an impact on my ability to move.

If I do realise I am in pain I can choose to do some stretching if it is muscle pain, move around if the pain is being caused by not enough movement or rest if the pain is caused by movement. If it is a headache I can take some pain relief if that would help, or I can rest, or take pain relief and rest.

If I realise I am injured I need to decide if it is an injury I can look after, or if I need medical assistance. It might sound odd, but I sometimes need help deciding if I need medical intervention because my pain response to injury is not typical- I have been told by doctors a bone can't be broken because I am not in enough pain, and the bone turned out to be broken, so I get someone who knows me well to help decide if I should get help.

Do you need to use the bathroom?

Yes, I am an adult. Yes, I don't always notice I need to pee until it's pretty urgent. Sometimes I feel wonky because I need to use the bathroom.

Are you stressed?

I sometimes need to ask myself this and check for physical signs of stress, like hunched shoulders, clenched jaw and fidgeting or stimming, in order to determine if I am stressed. If I think I might be stressed I might need to do a thought inventory and see if I can identify anything that has been on my mind a lot over the past couple of days to determine what the stress is (unless it is something obvious like I have a looming deadline or the children are all sick, etc.).

Stress isn't always from something negative either, so if I think I am stressed I will need to also have a think about how I could manage my time and stress load for the next few days to alleviate the problem.

Are you experiencing sensory overload?

This happens as often as me feeling stressed and the checks for this are much the same as the checks above for stress, but if I can't identify thoughts that are stressing me I check the environment. Am I squinting from bright or flashing lights? Am I huddling to avoid a particular sensation on my skin or in anticipation of touch? Am I aware of any sounds or smells that are irritating me or making me feel gross?

The solutions here can vary: noise cancelling headphones, sunglasses, put on or take off a layer of clothing, move somewhere less crowded, turn down volume of tvs, music or other electronic devices, go home, go to my room and shut the door, get in bed under the blanket and cocoon for a bit, go outside. What I choose to do will depend on the source of the overload, where I am, what I am doing, and who else is around.

Are you tired?

I don't always sleep well. Sometimes it's because the kids aren't sleeping well, but sometimes it's because of one of my semi regular periods of sleep disturbance in which I just can't fall asleep at night. I've become more relaxed about these times over the years and learned to go with the flow during my less sleep times, but I still need to be reminded that when they are happening I should allow myself more rest during the day so I don't burn out.

Sometimes I find it easier to go to sleep during the day, but won't think to do it unless I am prompted. I also don't always notice I am tired, as 'tired' and 'sleepy' aren't always the same thing for me…. so I don't think to lie down to sleep unless I am feeling sleepy, but it is possible to go to sleep without being sleepy if I am tired enough.

I have found that the most reliable way to figure out if I am tired enough to sleep is to lie down with my eyes closed for a while, so if all the above checks haven't fixed my feeling wonky, sometimes the best thing to do is go lie down and see what happens. With the children around I can't always do this, but there have been times I have and been surprised to find I then slept for hours and could still sleep that night.

Are you unwell, or becoming unwell?

I check this because it can be a good prompt to slow down for a few days. It's not always possible to tell if I am becoming unwell, but I do a check for sore throat and ears, headache, body aches, swollen glands, temperature, etc. If I think I am unwell or might be becoming unwell I try to give myself more rest and I set alarm reminders to eat and drink and take any necessary medication to make sure I look after myself.

Are you feeling wonky for more than one reason?

It's not uncommon for me to have more than one of the above things needing attention all at the same time. It's also not uncommon for it to be pretty difficult to choose which one to address first.
For me, if I realise I need to deal with more than one thing I usually do it in this order:
1. use the bathroom
2. eat
3. manage pain
4. reduce sensory stimulation
5. make a plan to manage stress
6. rest or sleep if possible

There is a lot of trial and error and experimenting involved in developing a list like this for yourself, and mistakes and misjudgements were definitely made along the way as I have refined my process of self care for wonky days. I still tweak it from time to time as I learn more about myself or notice that my tolerances have changed. It's all part of being a work in progress!

rest

For me there is a fine balance of activity and rest needed when I am recovering from the overwhelm of having done too much or pushed myself too far.

I manage my need for sensory, emotional, and mental regulation by ensuring I get a good mix of activity and rest, stimulus and deprivation.

In my daily life this involves:
-staying home, music, weighted blanket, and sitting or lying down for rest,
-noise cancelling headphones, sunglasses, darkness, and text for communication (with phone screen light set on low) for deprivation,
-spending time with friends, walking in locations I enjoy, reading articles, writing, taking photos, and karate training for activity and stimulus.

And there are the things I have to do, like feed myself, personal care tasks, housework and caring for my children.

Most of the time I organise things pretty well and the balance is maintained by my regular schedule.

When I am recovering from overwhelm I need to be fairly careful what I do for activity and stimulus because if I choose incorrectly I prolong my time of overwhelm.

For example, even though I would benefit the physical movement, sometimes the social aspect of attending karate training would make my attendance counterproductive. The social would drain more energy than is worth the benefit I gain from movement based sensory regulation. Sometimes I have to choose not to do something I want to do so I can recover in time to do things I have to do.

At the same time, if I rest and avoid input for too long, I risk prolonging my recovery by causing an imbalance due to not enough activity. Inertia due to inactivity causes sensory dysregulation too, and can be very difficult to pull myself out of.

Caring for an autistic mind and body means there is no point benefiting in one way while pushing myself too far in another direction when I am recovering. I can do those sort of things when all is in balance to start with, but not when I am recovering.

Understanding this about myself has led to a significant reduction in the frequency of both meltdown and shutdown for me. I don't always choose the best option, and sometimes that only becomes obvious after the fact! But I am getting better at looking after myself in this way.
I don't enjoy making decisions to miss out on things, but I have learned that patience with myself and my body's limitations is necessary.

flow

When I say
"I'm learning to go with the flow of my
neurodivergent brains natural rhythms"
it sounds kind of cool and self awareness-y and stuff.

***

But the reality of letting your brain flow through
weeks of minimal sleep at a time
when life is busy,
and the world expects things,
and children need to be fed and safe,
and there are things you want to do on top of the things you need to do,
and your body is doing odd medical things you don't understand
just to keep things interesting,
then it's not so cool,
it's more like frustrating and shit.

***

Because it's ok to just let your brain do its thing of being super super busy
and not sleeping much if there is nothing else in life to consider,
but that's not how it actually works.
And knowing that this is just part of a cycle
and that it will end when my brain is done processing all its busy thoughts
and my feelings will settle down when they have run their course
and I can go back to getting enough mental down time for my body to get into functioning in some sort of organised and productive way some time
is not comforting yet because I can't sense the slow down beginning
so I don't now how much longer it will be
and I'm tired.

***

This is what I mean when I say autism is a disability.
This is what I mean when I say being autistic doesn't mean I am disordered,
but it does mean there are things I can't do
because the world is not run in ways that best suit my living style.
This is why I have to become comfortable identifying as a disabled person.

***

This cycle of minimal sleep I go through a few times a year
is a pattern I recognise now,
but it doesn't make it any more possible to react to it any differently.
I have to ride it out.
I can't stop it from happening by doing anything or by worrying about it.
I have learned not to fight it,
but it is not easy knowing that for the next while I will not get household tasks done with any efficiency,
I will not be able to finish tasks I had on my to do list,
I won't even be able to write much of use because organising my thoughts is so hard-
ironic since the cause of the sleeplessness seems to be processing thoughts.

***

As a bonus when I don't sleep well my sensory system is more easily overloaded.
I will respond more negatively to touch, light and sound than usual.
I will find it more difficult to process language to offer words to others.

I will find it more difficult to process language to receive meaning from others.
I will feel ashamed.
I will want to hide away.

***

There is no support for me in moving through this.
This is the part of disability that people want us to just deal with quietly and alone.
This is not just me, I know my experience to be true for others as well.
We smile when we see you and say "good thanks" and move on with our day.
But "good thanks" is a way to protect ourselves from
your criticism born of not understanding.

***

So, I am saying:
I'm not always okay when I seem okay, but that's not bad.

***

This is autism as a disability in someone who was told
they are too high functioning to be officially diagnosed.

The world may not want to recognise me, but I know who I am.
I am myself, and my brain is doing its thing.
It's not easy, but it's not bad.
It's not typical, but it's not wrong.
It just is.
I am going with the flow.

interests

For a couple of years my personal Instagram account was full of pictures of my garden, chickens, food I was growing, flowers. For a while there were lots of pictures of walls and gates and buildings with interesting lines and structures. Then places I walked in….pretty streets, beautiful vistas, and sunsets. These days it's mostly places I travel to for work and for fun. There are a lot of pictures of beaches in the past few years. I like Instagram, because it is a context in which people expect you to post images in themes or topics….. or, if we want to delve into pathologising my use of Instagram, "special interests".

My Instagram account is not unusual. There are plenty of other people who post solely about their gardens. Or chickens. Or horses. Or interiors. Or vintage homewares. Or rusty gate posts. Or whatever it is they love to take pictures of and share with other people who are also interested in the same things.

Being interested in something and wanting to share that interest with others who also enjoy it is really acceptable. Instagram is a perfect example of it. Instagram has done a great job of normalising it in social media. It's interesting. It's fun. It makes up a part of many people's self care activities. They take pictures and share them with others for the sense of happiness, wellbeing and community they gain from it. That is healthy, and it is not frowned upon.

So, why do we feel the need to look at an autistic persons self care activities and call them "special interests" in a tone that has a negative connotation?

When I was gardening a lot, most days I would go out into my garden at some point to just be there. I would also go out to feed and water chickens, weed and tend the garden, harvest food and other practical tasks. I love doing those things and would often end up losing track of time and staying longer than I probably should if was going to get through other things I need to do. I would also usually take some photos while I was out there. I often take photos that are actually images I've taken before. One summer I had over 100 images on my phone of the 10 sunflowers I grew. I don't know how many photos I had of my chickens. It's probably more than 1,000.

If I forgot to take my phone outside with when I go I feel really annoyed. I did't want to go back to get it because someone might have seen me and asked me to do something that would interfere with going back outside to enjoy the garden and take photos. Sometimes I would take a while to decide what to do- deal with the disappointment of not taking photos this time, or risk being interrupted to go get the phone.

I've been known to sit out in the rain to watch chickens if I am not ready to go back inside yet. I have spent so long out there I have become badly sunburnt, but not come in even though I can feel it happening.

I probably spent more money than I "should" have on my garden. I was often thinking of ways to improve it and make it better. It interrupted getting other things done. I got restless on days when the weather or other necessary tasks prohibits a good visit outside. If I had to do other things first, I looked forward to going out all day. I enjoyed it even if no one else is interested, but finding others who are interested made it more exciting.

If I was stressed, I would go out to the garden for a while to regroup. If I was having trouble thinking something through I would sit and plan for the next thing I want to do in the garden and often my brain felt better and could process the other things once I had done that. If someone asked me about my garden, or my chickens, I could talk for ages about it. If you came to my house and notice the garden you were likely to get a long and animated monologue about it (I did this when the real estate agent was here once!). If you ask me how my day was I had to be careful to not tell you what is happening in my garden because I know you probably didn't mean that.

Gardening definitely fit the criteria for what people call a special interest, and if an Autistic child engaged in an activity the way I did with my garden they would be called a special interest, and often people would try to discourage such intense focus on it.

To me, though, it was a hobby that provided opportunity for self care. It helped me feel better. It grounded me. It gave me pleasure. There was a wonderful flow of energy that moved through me when I was focussing on it. I felt productive when I engaged in work on my garden. I felt a sense of accomplishment when I saw my work producing food, life and beauty. It was good for me. It was self care. There is no need to give that a label that has a negative connotation. I miss it terribly, but life changed and so I had to change where I spent time.

Now I have other ways of self caring. They still involve taking lots of photos! When I travel my phone is always in my hand ready to capture the images that grab my attention. When I head out to nature to regroup and relax, my phone comes with me to take pictures of what I see. I hold sensory memories in those images. I often collect small mementos as I go.

My favourite place to be is at the beach. The way the water moves and sounds, the shape of clouds, the lines of rocks, the textures of rock pools, all draw me in and soothe me. I take so many photos there. Capturing those images and looking at them later helps me feel better. It grounds me. It gives me pleasure. There is a wonderful flow of energy that moves through me when I was focussing on it.

When I realised how I engage with my interests, it completely changed how I view my sons interest in spending time gaming online. When I acknowledged the benefits in my life of fostering this interest it helped me become comfortable with my daughter needing that new lego set now. That is not to say that he spends all his time online, or we go buy her the lego set immediately, or that I spend all day wandering the beach. Life is more than that. But we allow for those interests to be a part of our day without attaching anything negative to them.

I've learned not to feel shame in needing to engage in self care. There is no shame in having "narrow interests" or "engaging in repetitive behaviours". I do these things and nobody judges me for it. I love posting images of my travels and explorations to instagram because in that context it is completely socially acceptable to obsessively share pictures on the same topic over and over again, and there are others who enjoy it when I do.

It has been so important to accept my interests as healthy and useful ways of being, and to find contexts in which they are valued and can be shared with others who share the same loves. It is a part of my self care that allows me to have the energy to do all the things I have to do and to stay healthy.

indistinguishability

All my life I have wanted to blend in. I have wanted to be understood, to feel safe, to be able to tolerate a bit of vulnerability without needing to retreat for days to recover, and to be accepted for who I am. I have tried so hard to look the part, talk the talk, be one of the gang. It's possible people do actually perceive that I have achieved that, but in my mind I have not. I have always still felt on the outside and uncomfortable, no matter what I have done to fit in.
I don't think I am the only person to feel this way. I don't even think this is something unique to neurodivergent people. I think it is something that is common all over the world, and it is perpetuated by our capitalistic society.

We are bombarded with teasers that tell us we need this, or that, or the other thing, in order to be up to date, cool, trendy, accepted and ultimately to be happy. We need to have the thing, be the thing and look like the thing to be considered right. The goal of these teasers is to get us to spend money (that we often don't have), and often it works, but there is another outcome that is much more dangerous than consumerism.

Our desire to be accepted, fuelled by society's reinforcing message that we must fit in at all costs, is creating an environment in which it is normal to modify ourselves in order to feel good about ourselves. We believe that if we can just look, act and be like everyone else it will solve our problems. We will be accepted. We will be happy. Everyone wants to be happy.

What we fail to acknowledge is that there is an internal incongruence created every time we change ourselves to suit others expectations. There is another chip taken out of our personal integrity every time we do something simply to fit in, when we would rather do what we are comfortable doing. We lose more of our own identity each time we conform, and we unwittingly become part of the problem that is growing generations of insecure and self loathing individuals all pretending to be overjoyed with their lives.

It is a sad thing to realise, that so many of us have bought in to the idea that blending in is desirable, when really there is nothing wrong with diversity.

It is a frightening thing to realise that as a result of this there are now entire industries reliant on this mentality and exploiting it in order to take money from parents in exchange for normalising their children. We see it in shops, in after school activities, clubs of all kinds, in our education system and in the medical profession.
It is hard enough to deal with as a typically developing child, who actually does have some capacity to engage with whatever the current accepted normal is. It has the potential to be life destroying if you are a disabled person who simply cannot mimic the majority determined normality.

As you read that last paragraph, please understand that I am in no way saying that anyone should have to conform, but that for those who simply cannot, for those who watch others engaging in this discourse, for those to whom the acquisition of acceptance by normality is unobtainable, the lure of indistinguishability- no matter how harmful it is- is strong and it is pervasive.

As adults, even when we realise the harm it does to us, we often still struggle to ignore the pull to conform. When, as a child, we desire to fit in, and on top of that know that our parents want us to appear normal just like our peers, we will likely do anything we can make it look like we have achieved that goal. No matter what the cost is to us.

As an Autistic parent to Autistic children, I often think about what messages I am sending my children. Whether they are neurodivergent or not, we parents need to be careful to nurture our children's unique characters and personalities. The health of their minds and spirits is much more important than society's push for conformity. We have all felt the incongruence of lost integrity as adults, and the responsibility lies with us do everything in our power to protect our children from experiencing it.

My words and actions as a parent are powerful, and I can use them as a safety net for my children, or I can use them to dangle the lure and trap them into believing they will never be acceptable until they do not look like themselves any more. I not only have to be careful how I talk to them about themselves, but I have to be careful what I model to them in my own choices, habits, and behaviour. It's a huge motivator for me to look after myself well when I realise that I am modelling to my children whether or not they should strive for individuality and living in ways that re healthy for them, or whether I model striving for indistinguishability.

crying

I cried in the supermarket.

The vanilla rice pudding I buy wasn't there. It's a food I keep on hand during times I know I am going to be busy and likely tending toward overwhelmed. I keep it available because I know I can always eat it.

When you have an autistic sensory system, eating can be difficult. On days when I am tired, overwhelmed and sensory sensitive, putting another unpredictable input into my body in the form of food is just too much. I would sometimes rather experience the discomfort of feeling hungry than I would deal with the taste and texture of a food that is not quite right.

My vanilla rice pudding is just right for those moments. It is sweet, but not too strong tasting. The flavour and texture are always the same. I don't have to do anything to prepare it. It never makes me feel ill. It doesn't add to my experience of sensory overwhelm. Sometimes a same food is a need for me. And yesterday the food I needed wasn't available, and I cried.

Honestly, it's not the first time I've become teary in the supermarket. Shopping is so difficult at the best of times. The noise, the brightness and complexity of the visual environment, the smells, and the intensity of the decision making! Even if I'm not tired, overwhelmed, or stressed when I begin, I will be by the time I'm finished.

I think most of the problem that day was that I couldn't make any more decisions, and so I got stuck not knowing what to do when my planned purchases were interrupted. Decision fatigue is fairly common for autistic people too. A combination of tiredness induced executive function funkiness and sensory overwhelm is a leading cause of meltdowns.

I didn't have a full blown meltdown that day in the supermarket, but that's because I was aware enough of my tiredness to know I shouldn't try to solve the problem then and there, but to just get myself home as quickly as I could. It's been many years of learning to understand myself to get to a point of knowing when not to push myself any further.

I have needed a lot of support to learn these things about myself. I needed help to figure out what the need is behind my tears and meltdowns. I needed that help given without shaming or expression of frustration that we I was making anyone else's life difficult. to this day I sometimes need help to calm the internal chaos I experience, until I have enough insight to begin to do that for myself. Often, I need to hear the experiences of other autistic people to help with this process.

There is nothing wrong with crying. There is no shame in experiencing a meltdown. But feelings of shame and being in the wrong are common for Autistic people, and I battle them too. I am getting better at letting those feelings pass when they surface, but it can be hard work.

disabled

"I hope I don't make you uncomfortable by saying this. But- you don't seem Autistic."

I immediately wondered what I would have to look like for this person to take me at my word. Did I not look autistic because I was speaking confidently about a topic I know a fair bit about in front of a group of people? Maybe because they hadn't expected the person facilitating a workshop about supporting a disabled person to be Autistic?

And really, how does an Autistic person "seem"?

There are a lot of ways in which people process information in very binary ways. Something is either this or that, with very little room for overlap. We need to challenge this way of thinking.

I am both disabled and able bodied. The two aren't mutually exclusive. My understanding of what people mean when they say able bodied is someone who is not physically disabled. I am able bodied.

Being disabled does not only happen when someone is physically disabled. We can be disabled by environment, expectations, overwhelm, overstimulated sensory systems, challenges with executive function, inability to communicate the way most people do, and many other things.

We don't have to "seem" or "look" or "appear" disabled to be disabled. We can also be disabled in some situations on some days, and not so disabled on other days. We can even be more, or less, disabled by the same things on different days or with different supports or lack of them.

We really need to get active about challenging the assumptions made about disability in our society. We need to find ways to change the conversation. It is important to let people know that disability is common, and not always visible in the ways they expect.

I honestly don't mind answering questions about my experience. I actually enjoy talking with people who have a genuine desire to hear a different perspective and understand where I am coming from. I don't like it when people start a conversation to correct me, as this person wanted to. It didn't matter what I said to them, they persisted with telling me labels were restrictive and bad and wouldn't let me speak to the fact that I found the self understanding gained with realising I am autistic truly liberating- they kept interrupting. In the end I just jotted down a couple of websites they could look at if they wanted to understand neurodiversity and the social model of disability better.

In this instance I found it very difficult to discuss because I wasn't prepared. I need to think about things and write them down to clarify my thoughts and develop scripts before I confidently respond in person to this sort of comment. I was better prepared the next time.
I had made a script for myself, and I've used it more than once.

"Disability doesn't always look how you expect it to. Not all disabilities are physical or observable just by looking. Sometimes you won't be able to see it at all, unless the person feels safe enough to disclose it to you either in words or behaviour. You definitely won't see what the person does in private to ensure their needs are met, and you likely won't notice many of the things they do to cope when they are in public. There is an issue of safety in disclosing disability in our society. Many of us hide our disability. When we disclose we are often not believed, or then presumed to be less competent than others. Many disabled people don't disclose because they understand society expects us to just get on with life without inconveniencing the non-disabled with requests for equality or having our support needs met. So, while I can understand your confusion over my disclosing my disability, it is based on misunderstandings arising from a society that routinely discriminates and makes it unsafe to disclose. But we are here, often getting our support quietly from each other in private communities we can only access after we receive the gift of a label that helps us understand ourselves."

identity

"The world will ask you who you are, and if you don't know, the world will tell you."
Carl Jung

I think about who I am regularly and often. I have considered my identity in terms of what I do, what relationships I keep in my life, what I think about, how I feel, my appearance… and all the things the world tells me are important! For a very long time, I only considered on my identity in terms of the ways the world told me I should.

Over the past few years though, I have been asking myself who I **am.**

It's a different question. Who am I. Not what do I do. Not who do I know. Not who do I spend time with. Not what do others say about me or think about me. No what do I think about. Not how do I feel.

Just. Who am I.

I haven't been able to decide!

Probably because identity isn't a fixed thing, or one that can actually be completely understood or confirmed.

I've had to learn to be comfortable with not knowing some things. And that is uncomfortable. Ironically.

And so I am getting closer to knowing.

Here's what I now think is important to know about identity.

Identity is not so much about doing, but about being. Identity is not determined by what you are told you are, or should be, by others.

Identity is what is inside you, that often others can't even see.

I've come to realise that other people actually cannot know who I truly am because they are not me. It is not possible to look at anything objectively. It is all subjective. When we look at each other we interpret everything through the lenses of our own selves, our own experiences, and our own assumptions and predictions.

In order to know yourself, you have to be able to look at yourself without placing too much value on what others opinions of you are. Especially when you are just imagining what their opinions are!

Knowing yourself takes incredible amounts of introspection done independently of others opinions. And the tricky thing for neurodivergent people who don't know they are neurodivergent is that knowing yourself when you don't even have the words available to you that can give you an accurate understanding is close to impossible. Which is why my understanding of my own identity has near on exploded in the past ten years. I finally had the words to be able to see myself more accurately.

My mind is nowhere near like Jungs in its capacity to theorise on personality, philosophy, archeology, literature, psychology, psychiatry and religion. But I do know that without the right frameworks we can't reach a point at which we can understand ourselves well enough to live healthy lives.

The world shouts at us every day with distracting messages about who we should want to be. But the answer isn't there. It is in us.

If we want to know who we are, if we want to develop a strong sense of identity, we have to be ready to look at ourselves, our whole selves. The things we like and the things we don't like. We have to be willing to like some things about ourselves that the world will tell us we should be ashamed of. We have to be confident enough to be able to recognise when the world is wrong. And it will be. Often.

We have to be able to say that we don't want the world to tell us who we are. And be genuinely convinced of it.

As neurodivergent people, for me as an autistic woman, we… I… have to build our identity on what we know for ourselves about ourselves that will work for us because of who we are.

Jung also said, "How can I be substantial if I do not cast a shadow? I must have a dark side also if I am to be whole."

Unfortunately, sadly, neurodivergence easily becomes part of our "shadow" if we pay too much attention to the world. Part of my healing, part of what has helped me to build my identity and become confident and comfortable with myself, is making peace with all the neurodivergent parts of me that the world tries to tell me to be ashamed of.

We cannot carry shame with us and still live our lives well.

Being autistic is part of my identity, and I will not be ashamed of it.

authentic

"Just be yourself", they say.
"Be proud of who you are."
"Everyone has something to offer."
"Be fearlessly authentic."

But, when I am authentic in my neurodivergent way, I see a pattern of becoming distant from friends and isolated from community. So, obviously, there are still rules about what you are allowed to do and what is considered valuable when you are being your proud authentic self.

My authentic neurodivergent self needs a lot of time alone, yet I crave connection with others.

My authentic neurodivergent self prefers to process language in writing rather than spoken word, especially if the thoughts I am processing involve a lot of emotion.

My authentic neurodivergent self relies heavily on social media as a form of communication, socialisation and finding supportive community.

My authentic neurodivergent self has executive functioning challenges that mean I can't engage in work tasks or house keeping tasks in ways that most would consider conventional.

When I am engaging with the world at large, the world that expects me to be authentic but only in ways considered typical, I have tried my best to engage in ways that are accepted, but find I am usually overwhelmed, exhausted and very aware of what the world sees as my inadequacies.

When I am engaging with my neurodivergent peers with my own brand of neurodivergent authenticity I do not feel the pressure to be a particular way or comply with a set of unspoken rules. I can communicate my thoughts and feelings in ways that are comfortable to me and in my own timing without fear of criticism or judgement.

As a result of having the weight of the worlds expectations removed from me by my friends in the safe space of neurodivergent community, I have been able to give myself permission to drop those expectations from myself.

So, I made the decision to show my neurodivergent authenticity to the world. It was, and continues to be, one of the hardest things I have ever done.

I spent 40 years of my life working to fit in, so learning to be comfortable not fitting in is neurodivergent authenticity.

I am aware that if I "just be myself", I will do things others don't understand and that may well leave them feeling uncomfortable, but that doesn't mean I should be excluded. What it actually means is that I have just made myself vulnerable and the people around me have decisions to make about how they will respond to that.

I know from experience that I will be laughed at for expressing pride in myself for achieving something it would never occur to others is even remotely difficult, so expressing that pride anyway is neurodivergent authenticity. It can be uncomfortable expressing my pride to others who don't acknowledge their privilege as a non disabled person who may not understand that my efforts are real even if they wouldn't find the thing I did worthy of celebrating for themselves.

I know that to many people the offer of "I'm here- If you want to talk, just text me anytime" is not as valued as "let's hang out and chat". So maintaining boundaries around how much time I can spend in face to face verbal conversation, and dealing with the resulting loss of friendship and contact with people, is neurodivergent authenticity.

Not everybody is prepared to accept and appreciate the diversity of what disabled people offer, instead of overlooking them for people who conform to their expectations.

For me, even though it has become easier over the years, it is still not possible to be fearlessly authentic, because I know I am judged as being less than for doing it. I've heard it said that bravery isn't the absence of fear, but the ability to do, even while fearful.

So I am still determined to be authentic, whether my proud authentic neurodivergent self is palatable to others sense of normality or not. For now I will be bravely authentic, and I will persist, because I believe people should be fearlessly authentic , and so I take on the responsibility for helping to create a world in which diversity is valued and being authentic is not an act of defiance or something that requires bravery.

www.ingramcontent.com/pod-product-compliance
Lightning Source LLC
Chambersburg PA
CBHW072338300426
44109CB00042B/1781